HOW TO AVOID THE

C*R*A*P

IN YOUR SEARCH FOR EMPLOYMENT!

(Click, Review, Apply & Pray)

**Job Hunting Intel for
Veterans Like You!**

By

Tom Stein, USMC Retired,

CCMP

&

Greg Wood, CCMP

www.TheHireTarget.org

C*R*A*P – Clicking, Reviewing, Applying & Praying

HOW TO AVOID THE

C R A P

IN YOUR SEARCH FOR EMPLOYMENT!

(Click, Review, Apply & Pray)

**Job Hunting Intel for
Veterans Like You!**

By

Tom Stein, USMC Retired, CCMP
Greg Wood, CCMP

Copyright Tom Stein and Greg Wood, 2016, All Rights Reserved

ISBN 10: 1500513989
ISBN 13: 9781500513986

Unless otherwise expressly noted, none of the individuals or business entities mentioned herein has endorsed the contents of this eBook.

Feel free to forward this as a PDF or printed copy to fellow Military Families, Veterans, and job seekers! Just make sure you give credit to the authors for quotes ;)

Disclosures and Disclaimers

Sorry, but <u>no one</u> — including the author and publisher — can guarantee you a job or any particular job. Your success will depend on numerous factors outside our control including, but not limited to your effort, experience, education, location, and match to an employer's needs.

While care and diligence have been taken in preparing the information contained herein, neither the authors nor the publisher guarantees its accuracy. It is sold and used by the reader with the understanding that the authors, contributors, publisher, and sales outlets are not engaged in rendering legal, financial or other professional advice. The reader is provided with guidelines, strategies and ideas that may or may not be applicable or appropriate for the reader's situation.

Laws and practices vary from state to state and if financial, legal or other technical expertise or assistance is required, the services of an experienced and competent professional should be sought. The author, contributors, and publisher specifically disclaim any liability that is incurred from the use or application of the contents of this book and system.

This book and the related materials are adapted from The Hire Road™ job search tutorial developed by the author, Greg Wood, CCMP, and proven in over eleven years of use by individuals, small businesses, corporations, and trainers worldwide.

The Hire Tactics™ Book Series

Strategic Job Search for Military Veterans!

The Hire Tactics™ (above) is available in paperback and eBook
format through Amazon and your nearest bookstore,
and includes all four individual eBooks!

The Hire Tactics™ individual eBook series

Welcome to The Hire Tactics™, the best-selling book dedicated to helping military veterans succeed in their job search mission. This edition combines all four individual books in the series, and they are designed to be short and sweet, so veterans can quickly begin using this proven job search approach. These books (described below) are available in eBook format through both Amazon.com and BarnesandNoble.com. The paperback edition of The Hire Tactics™ is available through Amazon.com and your nearest bookstore, while the eBook edition is also available through Amazon.com.

Book One — *"VETERAN EMPLOYMENT TACTICS! — Packaging Yourself for Job Hunting Success"* The first book in The Hire Tactics™ series introduces you to several innovative tools that will clearly separate you from your competition. In this book, you will learn how the job search system really works and how to use your tactical advantage as a military veteran!

Book Two — *"FIRE YOUR RESUME! — Tactics for a Successful Job Search in the New Economy"* The second book in The Hire Tactics™ series is one of our most popular. In it you will learn how to avoid turning a job search into C-R-A-P (Clicking, Reviewing, Applying and Praying). Learn why it is mission critical to get the Intel and package it so you can successfully penetrate the hidden job market. Learn how to educate employers about the value of your service and values you bring as a military veteran!

Book Three — *"LOCK AND LOAD! — 24 Job Interview Questions Military Veterans Need to Know!"* Being asked to take an interview means you are 80% of the way to accomplishing your mission. The interview is where you "seal the deal" and preparation is the key to success! In the third book in The Hire Tactics™ series you'll learn how to demonstrate the value you bring to the table by conducting a tactical and strategic interview that will greatly enhance your chances of winning the job offer. Additional questions more general to all job interviews can be found in Greg Wood's book, "Nailed It!"

Book Four — *"PAY DAY! — Negotiating Your True Worth, Not Just a Salary"* Let's face it; military veterans are not used to negotiating their pay! A table from the Pentagon listing your rank and time in service pretty much sets your paycheck and benefits. In this fourth book in The Hire Tactics™ series, you'll learn how to evaluate whether or not a job is worth taking and then, if it is, how to negotiate the difference between what you're offered and your true worth to the organization.

The Hire Advantage™ Book Series

Strategic Job Search for Civilians

The Hire Advantage™ (above) is available in paperback and eBook
format through Amazon and your nearest bookstore,
and includes all four individual eBooks!

The Hire Advantage™ individual eBook series

Welcome to The Hire Advantage™, the best-selling book on the new job search reality for civilians. This edition combines all four individual books in the series, and they are designed to be short and sweet, so those in career transition can quickly begin using this proven job search approach. These books (described below) are available in eBook format through Amazon.com and BarnesandNoble.com. The paperback edition of The Hire Advantage™ is available through Amazon.com and your nearest bookstore, while the eBook edition is also available through Amazon.com.

Book One — *"PACKAGING YOU! — Standing Out to Be Outstanding. The New Job Search Reality"* In addition to a professional resume and cover letter (which *every* job seeker uses), the first book in the series introduces you to the tools you need to brand yourself so you can separate yourself from your competition.

Book Two — *"FIRE YOUR RESUME! — Tactics for a Successful Job Search in the New Economy"* Don't let your job search turn into C-R-A-P (Clicking, Reviewing, Applying, and Praying). Learn the strategies and techniques that can help you penetrate the hidden job market by broadcasting your value to the business community and not your need for a "job." Learn how to convince employers that you are THE choice to solve their problems and NOT a piece of paper with antiquated formatting.

Book Three — *"52 INTERVIEW QUESTIONS YOU NEED TO KNOW!"* The hiring manager already knows you can do the job because it's right there on your biography and resume. But you still need to differentiate yourself from the competition. The interview is where you "seal the deal" and preparation is the key to success! In the third book in the series, you'll learn how to demonstrate the value you bring to the table by conducting a proactive, strategic interview that will greatly enhance your chances of winning the job offer.

Book Four — *"NEGOTIATING YOUR TRUE WORTH!"* If you've been out of work for some time, you're obviously going to be feeling a great sense of relief when you finally receive a job offer. It can be tempting to accept the offer as is and start the job right away. In this fourth book in The Hire Advantage™ series, you'll learn how to evaluate whether or not the job is worth taking and then, if it is, how to negotiate the difference between what you're offered and your true worth to the organization.

For more information on strategic job search for civilians visit www.thehirechallenge.com

TABLE OF CONTENTS

ABOUT THE AUTHORS

Tom Stein, USMC Retired

Tom Stein is a business owner, experienced senior executive, author, and a public speaker. Prior to working in corporate America, Mr. Stein was a senior officer in the Marine Corps, specializing in Aviation, Information Technology, and Logistics. He is a graduate of the United States Naval Academy and holds numerous degrees and certificates in Aviation, Information Technology, and Education. As an executive program manager, he has held executive positions and designations in his fields of expertise and has worked with Fortune 100 companies like Apple, Dell, Ingram Micro, Targus, and Wal-Mart.

He has never lost touch with his military roots as he continues his passion for aviation as an Adjunct Professor and Mentor for Embry-Riddle Aeronautical University, where he has been a faculty and staff member since 1998. Mr. Stein instructs and develops programs for undergraduate and graduate students. Mr. Stein is also the former Chairman of the Board for the Orange County Veteran Employment Committee.

As a Certified Career Management Professional (CCMP), he continues to focus on assisting military personnel and veterans in their career search and transition. He teaches classes nationwide to assist veterans in transitioning from military to civilian careers.

To contact Tom for keynotes, corporate talks, training, and consultations:

Tom Stein
The Hire Target™
8502 E. Chapman Avenue, Suite #157
Orange, CA 92869
Office: (714) 356-2239
Tom@thehiretarget.org

A Service Disabled Veteran Owned
Small Business Owner (SDVOSB)
CAGE/NCAGE: 6KBY4

For more information on The Hire Tactics™ Job Search Tutorial:

www.TheHireTactics.com
www.TheHireTarget.org
www.TheHireChallenge.com

Greg Wood, CCMP

Greg Wood is a Certified Career Management Professional (CCMP), who has experienced firsthand the challenges and anxiety of being unemployed several times during his 30+ years of business experience. With more than thirteen years of experience in both outplacement and executive search, Greg earned his reputation as a pre-eminent career counselor through the creation of The Hire Road™, an innovative, strategic approach to job search. His unique program takes job seekers step-by-step through the entire job search process, providing all the resources and tools necessary to achieve differentiation and shorten their time in transition at a very critical time in their lives.

An excellent trainer and presenter, Mr. Wood is a frequent guest speaker at a variety of professional and career transition support groups across the nation. Greg's corporate background includes domestic and international experience in a variety of industries including executive search, publishing, high-technology and healthcare. He has held senior management positions with mid-size as well as major Fortune 500 corporations.

To contact Greg for keynotes, corporate outplacement, and one-on-one consultation:

Greg Wood
4340 E. Indian School Road, Suite 21
Phoenix, AZ 85018
Office: (949) 338-4124
Greg@thehirechallenge.com

For more information on The Hire Road™ Job Search Tutorial:

www.TheHireChallenge.com

INTRODUCTION

Does this picture sound familiar?

You've been out-of-work for several months and things are getting tight. Any severance money has long since run out, savings (if you had any) are dwindling or gone, but your expenses just keep increasing. Your power bill is creeping higher as the weather changes, gasoline is ridiculous, and food is more expensive than ever.

So you get up determined to find as many job opportunities as you can. You know the newspaper want ads are a joke, so you go online and start **CLICKING** on Internet job boards or target company websites that use online applications.

You **REVIEW** several good sounding opportunities and decide to **APPLY**. You upload your resume, answer questions about your experience, then answer the mandatory legal disclosures about ethnicity and then you hit "send," **PRAYING** this time will be different.

You click, review, apply and pray five, ten, maybe even fifty times in a single day. You keep following the recipe and doing the same thing, over and over again.

And each time after you hit send, you sit back and wonder why the phone's not ringing. Your resume shows that you are a perfect fit for that job, but you don't ever get a response. No return emails, no phone calls, NOTHING.

No way to even know they got your application!

Let's face it. The traditional approach to finding a job has turned to **C*R*A*P**...

Clicking, Reviewing, Applying, and Praying

If you're one of the 99.9% of job seekers who has been following this approach, you know <u>exactly</u> what we're talking about. You've gotten no results and you're frustrated, discouraged, probably a little angry, and don't know where to turn.

There is a huge pool of talent on the street, and the competition for each and every job is incredibly fierce. Clients who in previous years had offers lined up before leaving their previous job are going months without even a single interview.

And yet, we talk to Human Resources (HR) professionals all the time who tell me they're having a difficult time finding the right talent to fill their open positions! And at the same time, we're hearing from well-qualified job seekers who tell us they're having a hell of a time getting in front of a hiring manager for an interview, despite their "perfect resume and knock 'em dead cover letter."

We don't have to tell frustrated job seekers like you that something is wrong.

What's wrong is no one told you HOW the new digital job hunting world really works!

No one has shared the "dirty little insider secrets" to the REAL story behind using the Internet for job searches.

We want to share the cold hard facts about job hunting in the digital world.

You're facing competition from thousands of applicants worldwide, bogus job listings, come-on's and scams, out-of-date Internet job boards and company websites, unsolicited contacts from recruiters and salespeople trying to sell you job search related services, cumbersome online applications, scanning software that will kick you out in an instant if you fail to include the right keywords and, finally, overworked and underpaid personnel jockeys who, believe me, don't have a clue about the nature of the work to be done. They would much prefer to hit "delete" instead of briefly glancing at your resume for as little as fifteen to thirty seconds.

Go job hunting in the digital universe and you will get contacted by some of the worst vermin in the world. These "pond scum" have discovered that job seekers desperate for employment are easy targets. And they have just enough real offers to keep themselves out of jail. We hear complaints all the time about the con artists who promise the moon and give you nothing in exchange for your precious and limited money.

This is what you're up against.

The system as it now exists is a quagmire that you have to somehow try and navigate.

The whole system seems to have become C*R*A*P.

That's why we're here. We're here to help you avoid the C*R*A*P.

To succeed in your job search in our new economy requires creativity, a willingness to think outside the box, and innovative approaches to effectively meet the challenges of finding employment. Things have changed. Times have changed. And times are tough. You need new tools and new tactics for this new job reality.

Let's break down all the C*R*A*P to see why the traditional approach is not working for you:

CHAPTER ONE - "Clicking"

When we first start working with a client/veteran in transition, we begin by asking what they've been doing so far in terms of their job search activity. Over 90% tell me they primarily go to as many posted jobs as possible! They then look for anything that is even remotely close to what they can do. They then apply, apply, apply.

Sound familiar?

We know you probably hear the sound in your sleep…**click**…after **click**…after **click** in the hopes of finding that "perfect" job. You know the one…the one where your resume screams that you're the "perfect fit" for the job.

What you are really doing is nothing more than throwing a piece of paper up in the air hoping someone will catch it. You think your "powerful resume" is one in a million. Well, guess what? It is! It's *one of millions*!

Good luck with that approach.

Then there are the scams. Check out the comment posted by one of the job seekers I counseled. Comments like this are all over the Internet:

> *"About three days after posting my resume on Monster.com, I received two recruiting emails from well known companies. After rereading them (in slight disbelief) I realized that they showed many of the signs of your typical phishing scam. The jobs had been posted as a way to get information to steal my identity and who knows what else!"*

The problem is the ratio of bad guys to good guys is so lop-sided I now tell most clients to stay off the Job Boards! 99% of Internet sites offer nothing more than the usual C*R*A*P. But if you want to try them, here is more information on how you can use them safely.

JOB BOARDS

The first major **DIRTY LITTLE SECRET OF JOB HUNTING** is the majority of online job boards are REALLY in the business of resume preparation, interview training, and other "services" for job seekers, and SELLING your information to recruiters and network marketing companies. They are NOT really in the business of finding you a job!

Think about it. The job boards are free to you, so where are they making their money? There are more and more boards every day so they must be profitable and making money from somewhere!

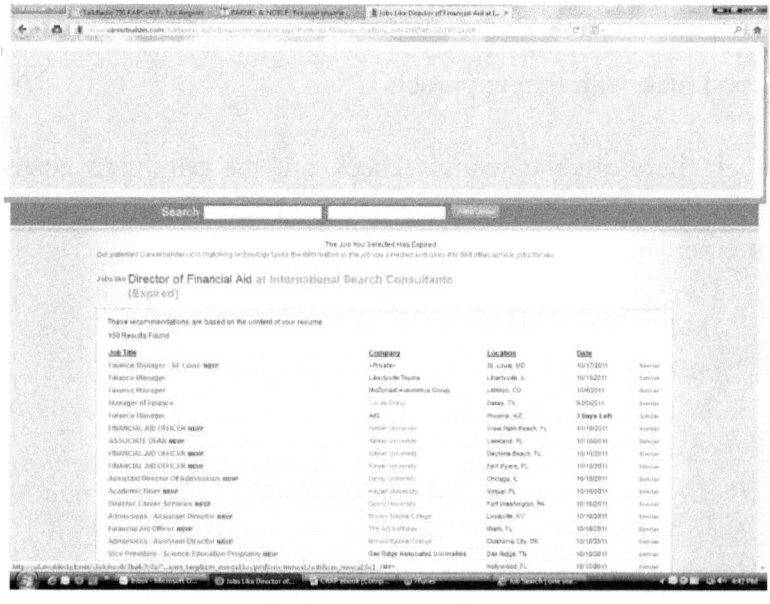

Did you know that when you blast your resume out to companies using a job board, it is very easy for them to track how often and how long you have been trying to use them to get a job? They have placed cookies on your PC or MAC that allow them to track every time you visit!

And let's get real; the operators of these boards are well aware how few, if any, of their users get a serious job response. Sometimes we think they deliberately frustrate their users so the lack of response gives the board owners a reason to tell you that something like your resume is the problem! Then they try to up-sell their "professional resume" writing services, job search training or their "special limited time only gold foo-foo package" and who knows what else to make a buck off your desperation and frustration with their useless job listings.

Oh, and don't be surprised if you start getting job offers from companies looking to train you to sell life insurance, do network marketing, work-at-home, attend a trade school, or recommend sign-up for webinars for all manner of "opportunities." Your information was SOLD to these companies as "warm leads" because they know a lot about you from your resume and applications. One of our clients told us she had to change her email address she was getting so many emails from insurance companies!

Then there are privacy issues. Not only does posting your resume open you up to privacy threats; your information (name, address, phone number, email) can be collected, stored and sold to third-party vendors, especially if you allow your resume to be searchable by any employer or recruiter.

So the time you spend posting to job boards is basically

wasted. The boards are more interested in selling you stuff than finding you a job!

COMPANY WEBSITES

The good news is that career pages on a company website are generally better than job boards, since they will probably not sell your information or try and sell you a resume writing service. But the second **DIRTY LITTLE SECRET OF JOB HUNTING** is this: the job opening you just saw is usually the <u>same listing</u> you will see again on half a dozen OTHER job boards! Most of the Internet job boards use search programs and part-time minimum wage staff to "scrape" job listings off company sites, newspapers, Craigslist and other locations to add to their inventory! After all, they want to have as large an inventory as possible to attract as many job seekers as possible.

The third **DIRTY LITTLE SECRET OF JOB HUNTING**: the bigger the company, the more likely they are to use a computer program called a "meatgrinder" to <u>eliminate</u> your uploaded resume before a human being ever sees it!

HR departments are inundated with resumes. The tough economy has increased the steady flow of applicants to a flood of resumes every day. And the online technology has let anyone with access to a computer send a resume to everywhere and anywhere they can, regardless of whether or not they are even qualified for the job. This has created a virtual tsunami of resumes to companies anytime they advertise a job!

So HR got smart. Almost ALL companies are now using scanning technology—not as a hiring tool—but as a <u>filtering</u> tool. If you have been online for job applications I bet you've undoubtedly noticed that many, if not all companies, <u>require</u> you to upload your resume online. And even if you send in a paper resume, most HR departments will simply scan it back into their system.

Once in the system, resumes are fed to a "meatgrinder" program that looks for keywords and phrases that match their job opening. And many of these keywords are NOT in the job description, so they can easily weed out anyone who isn't familiar with the job and/or the company and/or the industry.

If you are lucky (and that is a BIG "if"), you may make it into the short stack of prospects who had the right words in the right place. Then a human being from HR will scan the now shortened pile before contacting the candidates they like for an interview.

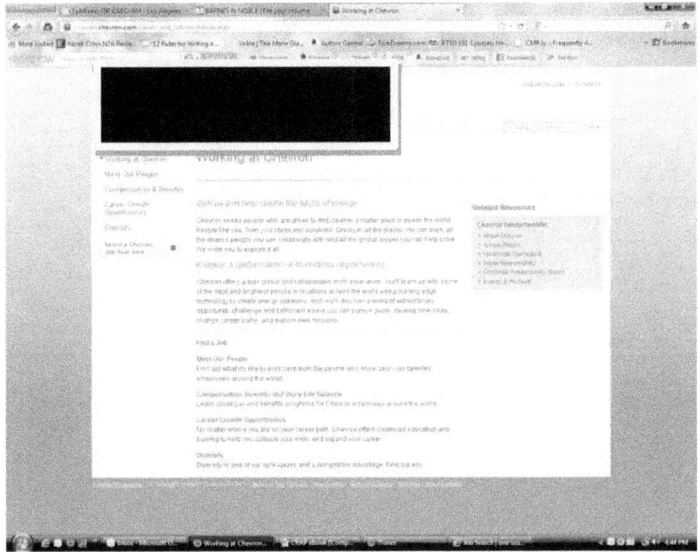

As you can see, these are long odds that you wouldn't play with real money. But job seekers do it every day, putting everything they have into such a long shot process.

CHAPTER TWO - "Reviewing"

As you forge ahead with your digital job search, with each click of your mouse comes a rush of excitement as you stumble upon the occasional job description that seems to be a match to your qualifications and experience. With so many job postings to **review** you're bound to find a job eventually, right?

As you continue to **review** dozens and dozens of job postings, consider these harsh realities when relying on company websites and job boards:

<u>Reality #1</u> — Many companies post jobs even though the positions have been filled! While the candidate may have already been chosen, the company still posts the job opening to comply with internal company policy or to abide by legal hiring practices.

<u>Reality #2</u> — The vast majority of job postings on company websites (and job boards) are written by HR personnel. They are poorly written and nothing more than a cursory overview of the job responsibilities and requirements. They tell you very little about the nature of the work to be done and nothing about the hiring manager or the people you'll be working with. As we say in career counseling, "Poor ads will ALWAYS attract poor candidates."

<u>Reality #3</u> — According to the most recent Source of Hire study by CareerXroads, job boards accounted for 25% of external hires companies made. This is a significant increase over prior years, where the percentage of external hires from job boards was considerably lower. This may sound encouraging to job seekers; however, the reality is **75% of open positions were filled by candidates from other**

sources. This same study listed the highest percentage of external hires coming from **referrals**. Where do you think you should you be spending the majority of your time?

<u>Reality #4</u> — The number of postings on Internet job boards has declined recently due to the economy and the fact that companies are not hiring. The competition, therefore, is even greater for those that are advertised.

<u>Reality #5</u> — To many individuals seeking work, job boards are seen as classified ads on steroids and the main source for finding employment. And yet, 99.9% of job seekers still don't get it: when 4,000 people apply for a single job, many times the most qualified candidates will slip through the cracks while someone in personnel is sifting through thousands of resumes. The result? The majority of time the wrong candidate is hired.

<u>Reality #6</u> — Many companies are known for posting "fake" jobs. They do this to drive a pipeline of candidate resumes to keep their inventory of candidates strong. Since many companies have agreements with major job boards like Monster, CareerBuilder, etc., they use these fake listings to gather resumes **for future needs**. If an employer has bought fifty job postings and only used forty, why not post fake jobs to gather resumes before the postings expire?

Rather than ignore posted jobs, we suggest you spend perhaps 20-25% of your job search time chasing them on the Internet. Another suggestion: www.indeed.com. This website brings all posted jobs together, from all job boards, company websites, and other sources. It's a great tool to save time and maximize your return.

CHAPTER THREE - "Applying"

Because of the overwhelming number of applicants, many companies are now using online applications as just another way to screen you OUT. These forms have to be filled out in full before you can even submit a resume.

A word of advice: mass distribution of your resume is a waste of time. Applying for hundreds of jobs over the course of several months is insane. *There aren't hundreds of jobs out there for you; only a select few.*

AGAIN — Stop with the **C*R*A*P!**

Let's assume you've finally found that "perfect" job on a company website or job board. After practically wetting yourself, you're ready to fire off your resume and wait for the invitation to come in for an interview. But, before you can, you need to complete the online application.

Here are the realities of online applications:

Online Reality #1 — No one is sitting and reading the applications as they come in. Software programs scan the completed form, looking for the right boxes to be checked, the right answers, the right keywords and phrases. If you don't have them, you're out of luck. Here's an example:

> *Online applications will often ask for your "Previous Salary" and/or "Desired Salary." Let's say the base salary range for the position you're applying for is $50,000 to $60,000 (although you probably won't know it at this point). If you list your "Previous Salary" as $30,000, the employer*

will think you're a lightweight and your application will be rejected. If you indicate your "Desired Salary" is $65,000, do you think there's a snowball's chance in hell that you'll be considered because the salary you want (and deserve) is outside their range?

Online Reality #2 — Many times companies build in disqualifiers to reduce the huge number of applications they receive. These can include specific degrees, years of experience, special skills with special equipment or programs, etc. This is done not because they believe a B.A. degree in Art History will help you be a better sales rep. They do it to thin down the applicant herd flooding the website!

Online Reality #3 — If your completed online application gets past the initial screening software, you're now at the mercy of some personnel jockey who's going to decide whether you're valuable enough to put in front of the hiring manager for an interview.

Applying online should be just one of the avenues you use in your job search, but not your only avenue.

Job boards? Your call as to whether or not you want to play in that sandbox now that you know what they can be like.

CHAPTER FOUR - "Praying"

You may or may not be religious; however, every job seeker we know resorts to some form of prayer when submitting applications and resumes. If you don't believe me, check out the Internet to see how many people have asked for prayers to help them with their job search and prior to their job interview. Religious or not, as a desperate job seeker you may well want to seek help from a "Hire Source."

The stark reality is that you face an enormous amount of competition. Job postings on company websites (and anywhere else on the Internet) are literally open to the world. Inevitably, the number of applicants for any posted job is going to be enormous. For example, a company in Irvine, California recently posted ONE job opening on its website. In just over a week they received over 4,000 resumes for that one posting! Maybe yours was one of them?

In today's digital job search you MUST consider YOUR odds.

As you now know, the traditional system of finding employment is **C*R*A*P**. It's a frustrating, discouraging exercise which can cause you significant emotional and physical stress.

Why?

Because you lack control.

Your entire approach to job search is reactive. You're WAITING for something to happen. You're WAITING for someone to do something. You're WAITING for someone to notice YOU.

You need to go…

From C*R*A*P to CONTROL

CHAPTER FIVE – "Control Your Search"

Go ahead and use the Internet but do it NOT as your primary job search and application tool, but as one of the ways to become a successful job HOLDER!

Avoid the **C*R*A*P** and take control.
You need to learn to be creative in your job search by working smarter, not harder.

Stop worrying about your employment and start thinking about your employability! Recognize that you ARE unique.

You possess skills, experience, and expertise which represent significant VALUE to the business community. However, also recognize that your value means NOTHING to an overworked, underpaid personnel jockey.

From HR's perspective, hiring has been reduced down to nothing more than keywords and phrases on a resume.

We can't totally blame them. There is no other way they can filter out a few potential candidates from the thousands of applications that will flood into their inboxes whenever they post a job. You can blame job seekers so desperate for a job they send in a resume or click and apply even when they are TOTALLY unqualified for the position (of course you've never done that hoping you'd somehow slip through, now have you?).

Stop wallowing in **C*R*A*P** and take the strategic approach to job search.

Quoting Greg Wood, "Broadcast your VALUE not your resume!"

Educate the business community about who you are and what you can bring to the table. Use your resume as backup, as reinforcement. Spend the majority of your time targeting *companies*, <u>not</u> jobs.

You need to become PROACTIVE.

You need to stop waiting on the call. What you need now is to change your mindset, set a strategy, and use better tactics.

And better tactics start with better information.
And where to you go for better information?
Yup, believe it or not, the digital world.

You are going to use the same Internet that has been causing you headaches and heartaches.

But now you are going to use it in a way that few, if any, job seekers will take the time and effort to learn! You are going to discover the keywords and other tactics needed to find a job.

Now we know it's easier to wake up on a Monday morning, make a cup of coffee, stagger over to the computer in your bathrobe, and start to scroll down job after job after job on Internet job boards and company websites. But, not being very hard also means not very productive because so many job seekers are taking that lazy way out!

Relying primarily (if not totally) on Internet job boards is a very frustrating and unproductive exercise. You need to realize the fierce amount of competition you face for each and every one of these posted jobs you apply for. Regardless of your qualifications, your odds of getting noticed are very slim to none.

So how do you improve your odds?

You CHANGE YOUR MINDSET to researching the job and its requirements.

You CHANGE YOUR WORK to researching jobs with the best match to your keywords and experience and minimizing the filters. For example, if the job description requires a degree and you do not have one, move on.

Stop **WAITING** for opportunity and start **CREATING** opportunity!

By following the traditional C*R*A*P approach you are *waiting* to get noticed. You're *waiting* for someone to find your submission and pick your resume out of the stack of THOUSANDS. You are *waiting* to be seen as better than the rest. You're *waiting* for something to happen. You are giving away your control and your power!

Stop waiting, stop whining, and start winning!

CHANGE YOUR FOCUS from waiting on someone to find your resume or application from the thousands online. Change your goal from getting your resume noticed in a pile of paper or emails to getting in *front* of the people who can see you are more than a chronological resume.

CHANGE YOUR FOCUS from complaining about how hard it is to find a job to securing an interview.

CHANGE YOUR FOCUS FROM getting a job to securing an interview.

STOP WORRYING ABOUT FINDING A "JOB" AND START THINKING ABOUT YOUR EMPLOYABILITY!

Your aim is not to find a job on the first pass! Your target is someone that can help you get an interview to see if you WANT to work at a location and if you are a good match!

CHAPTER SIX – Reorder Your Priorities

Now, we're not saying you should totally ignore online job searches. Not everything online turns into C*R*A*P. Sadly, most uninformed job seekers spend their time in this environment!

So go ahead and spend maybe 10% but no MORE THAN 20% of your time clicking and chasing online jobs because who knows, you may get lucky! Some job seekers do. There are just enough jobs found online to keep job boards from being hauled up on charges of fraud.

However, recognize the odds are against you. They are REALLY against you if you're relying totally on the Internet to find your next job.

Instead, spend the rest of your time, at <u>least</u> 80%, building on what is it that makes you employ*able*. This means research and *networking*.

Instead of chasing jobs, start thinking about the kinds of companies you'd like to go to work for. Decide what geographical areas you'd like to work in and how far you're willing to commute to get to a job.

Will you move?
How big a company must it be?
How much traveling?
What kind of work environment – laid-back or button-down?
9-to-5 or flexible, long hours?
Rigid chain of command (like the police) or loose teams?
What are the opportunities for advancement, benefits, etc.?
Determine all the critical factors for your life when you get a job. How flexible are you? What is important, what is "nice" and

what is non-negotiable and what is a must-have? What will you compromise over and what is a deal breaker?

Then begin to research companies of interest to you within that defined scope.

At this point, as you go through this exercise, you don't care whether your targeted companies are hiring, firing, upsizing, side winding, or downsizing.

Your #1 priority is to find out more about as many companies as you can that fit your criteria.

Whether or not they have jobs comes *later*.

I bet you are saying to yourself – that's backwards! I'll worry about all those details <u>AFTER </u>I get a job offer.

That's what EVERYONE ELSE DOES! That is the STANDARD tactic and strategy of find an open job, apply alongside a herd of people and hope you stand out!

These are new times with new job realities. You MUST think outside the box to win this battle! You MUST use a different approach if you want to be found and get the best job for you!

Once you know what you want in detail, your assignment is to find the employers that have your perfect job! Tell everyone you know what kind of company you are looking for. **WARNING**: DO <u>NOT</u> ASK CONTACTS FOR A JOB OR WHO IS HIRING!!!!!!!!!!!!

Here is the secret to success: Just use the following phrase:

"Who do you know who…?"

For example, "Who do you know who works on heads-up displays for aircraft?"

"Who do you know who trains emergency medical technicians?"

"Who do you know who has expertise in logistics?"

You want to find contacts that do what you want to do where you want to do it! You want to talk to a real person about what they do and see if you might want to do it too.

Most job seekers will be asking for a job and put the other person on the spot by asking "who has a job" or even worse "are YOU hiring?" Using the phrase "who do you know who" gives the person you are talking with a way out and puts no pressure on them. You are asking for a referral, NOT a job.

Interestingly, most people asked "who do you know who" will often be the "who" you are looking for! That is especially true if you're smart in your networking efforts!

Use all kinds of networks; both online and real world! Go to Chambers, trade associations, meetups, and special groups for veterans like the VA. Go everywhere and anywhere that people with your job type may congregate. Create a list of contact information such as phone numbers and email addresses for each one.

Learn what you can about those companies. Read their websites, Google them. Search for local news and announcements. Check finance sites for news about them. Check what kind of jobs they may have posted. Figure out what skills, experience, knowledge, and strengths you have that may uniquely fit their organization. Use the news section of the local paper or Internet search to see what new projects, contracts or issues they may have that you can help solve for them.

Your goal is to talk with as many people as you can about your dream company NOT your dream job!

CHAPTER SEVEN – You're In!

This book is designed to give you the Intel you needed to avoid the C*R*A*P that destroys the momentum and dreams of many Veterans looking for jobs!

It is designed to help you focus on using successful tactics proven to find you the **opportunity to be interviewed** for a good job that rewards you for your service to this country.

This book was NOT designed to be a complete system or provide all the steps in the Four Job Search Milestones*. We designed this book to help as many Veterans as possible avoid the heartache and frustration we see every day from discouraged online job seekers.

PLEASE avoid the **C*R*A*P**!

Do your homework to find the companies you would like to work at. Ask, "Who do you know who?" Use the Biography, Management Endorsements, and Post-Interview Packet to separate yourself from the competition and dramatically improve your odds for getting that job offer. Practice your interview questions and then know how to negotiate your future paydays.

With better tactics and strategies, you WILL win the battle and find the job your service has prepared you for!

GOOD HUNTING!

*Note - These innovative tools and related strategies can be found in The Hire Tactics™ Job Search Tutorial, the most comprehensive, yet affordable, career transition resource on the market today for our Military Families!

YOU'RE HIRED!

THE Hire Tactics™ Job Search Tutorial

(https://thehireadvantage.com/?set_package =military)

Also available in a CD version

We know some of you may need more help than just this book. We also know you may not have access to the resources you need if you are deployed or live in an area without nearby access to VA resources. So if you serious about changing your mindset and implementing the tactics we've described in this book then The Hire Tactics™ Job Search Tutorial may be your answer.

In addition to showing you how to prepare the critical new tool of a Biography, the program introduces other innovative tactics and strategies such as Management Endorsements, the Post-Interview Packet and the 80 plus question Audio Interview CD, all to help you stand head and shoulders above your competition!

Learn the language of the civilian job search protocols and rehearse them. Get templates and samples of biographies and the necessary professionally-written resumes and cover letters.

To learn more visit

www.thehiretarget.org or www.thehirechallenge.com

Testimonials for THE HIRE ROAD™ and THE HIRE TACTICS™ Job Search Tutorials

Here are just a few comments from job seekers who have taken The Hire Tactics and the The Hire Road™ approach:

"Tom Stein's and Greg Wood's *The Hire Tactics!* was the most influential book I read in preparing for my transition to a second career after over two decades of military service. As I embarked on my transition journey, I was nervous, anxious, fearful, overwhelmed, and excited all at the same time. *The Hire Tactics!* not only calmed my emotions, it focused my time and efforts on the target of landing my dream job. Tom and Greg gave me the tactics for a successful military transition and entry into Corporate America. Most importantly, they taught me how to market myself, my brand, and the importance of differentiating myself from the competition.

The Hire Tactics! was the force multiplier that resulted in me landing my new career with my employer of choice from the start! Thank you Tom and Greg; due to your expert insight and guidance I wake up energized and excited each morning and could not be happier with my second career! My advice to other veterans: Get your hands on a copy of *The Hire Tactics!* today."

> *Michael DeWitt, USAA Financial Foundations,*
> *Former Commanding Officer, US Navy*
> *Phoenix, AZ*

"*The Hire Road* is the most comprehensive and direct in utilizing a realistic approach in the pursuit of employment. I think your product is an excellent tool for job seekers…especially military personnel. I would highly recommend it to my fellow Marines."

> *N. L.*
> *MGySgt/USMC/Ret*
> *Los Alamitos, CA*

"I think *The Hire Road* program should become part of the workforce development system as an added feature available in the One Stop Career Centers throughout the United States. I highly recommend this product."

Jim McShane, Public Administrator, Illinois Active in the Workforce Investment Act Illinois (WIA) System

"I thought the material was good and provided good direction for those just getting out of the military. The material kick starts the thought process and provides insight to many things military people may not think about as they exit the service. The program provides good organization and processes for how to go about transitioning into the private sector."

Chris Rogers, Major USMC.
Orange County, CA

"I found *The Hire Road* extremely helpful. I've even passed it along to several friends who were interested in how I went about my job search.

The interview strategies I learned and the writing techniques demonstrated in the letter templates were pivotal to my transition into my current role. The interview process was long and rigorous, so having an arsenal of different angles for answering questions in my pocket was extremely helpful! In particular, I liked listening to the CD in the car on the way to interviews - it helped get me into the right mindset."

Hayley Chilton, Former Graduate Student, Cal State San Luis Obispo (SLO), Marketing Manager, Medical Device Industry

"I had the pleasure of meeting Greg about a month ago and learning about the job search strategies he teaches with *The Hire Road*. In the space of those 4 weeks I have been actively applying *The Hire Road* resources and strategy for communicating added value to potential employers. In that short time, I received three invitations for interviews with hiring managers of companies I was most interested in! This week I was offered a position at one of these companies which I gratefully accepted. Although the outcome speaks for itself, it was the process of getting there with Greg's help for which I am most THANKFUL. I appreciate that Greg not only gave me the resources, but he helped me to use them with the most impact. I am humbled and grateful for within four weeks of being suddenly unemployed, I have what looks like will be a great job."

Ron Sato
Santa Ana, CA

"*The Hire Road* was pivotal in my search for new employment, giving me all the professional tools necessary to maximize my employment search, prepare for interviews, and create a post interview presentation of myself, all of which enabled me to stand out from the competition and land the perfect job. I would recommend Greg and *The Hire Road* to anyone who is looking to put all the integral pieces of a new employment search together."

Leslie Rush
Oceanside, CA

"Greg is an excellent teacher and an inspirational role model. He is empowering while sharing his knowledge and motivates job seekers to test his unique techniques in real life. Greg has been a great supporter throughout the process, providing practical advice and hope. I highly recommend Greg's services to all on the road to success."

Klara Detrano
Costa Mesa, CA

"*The Hire Road* was very effective and helped shorten my time between jobs. The seminar is a welcome change from the standard advice found in numerous books and tapes, especially the approach to interviewing. I'm sure the strategies will be just as valuable if and when I find myself in transition again".

Larry Weimann
St. Louis, MO

"*The Hire Road* has led to spectacular results. I have used the techniques provided on the CDs and achieved results that I could never have gotten using other methods. The recommendations in *The Hire Road* definitely got me noticed and helped me feel more confident in my interviews. Thank you for providing this very helpful job search tool."

Robert Lee
Simi Valley, CA

"I did use *The Hire Road* program. The CDs and the DVD were great. I have had three job offers, accepted one last week, and started Monday."

Jason Stone
Alpharetta, GA

"*The Hire Road* really gave me the help I needed. I went into the interview with a lot of confidence and got the offer!"

Susan Cole
Indianapolis, IN

"*The Hire Road* was an instrumental part of beginning my job search. The in-home seminar turned the anxiety of the interview into a position of knowledge and confidence. I am very happy to have made the choice to go with *The Hire Road* and I have nothing but praise for their techniques, knowledge and strategies."

Robert King
Whittier, CA

Attention Military Families!

Currently unemployed? Military spouse? Still serving, but looking for a change? Reentering the job market? The Hire Tactics™ job search tutorial utilizes video, narratives and animation to present tools and techniques that will help you stand out from the competition and assist in your journey from military to civilian employment!

Get the Civilian Job & Pay
Your Service Deserves!

For more information, please visit:

www.thehiretarget.org or www.thehirechallenge.com

NOTES

VISIT YOUR FAVORITE BOOKSELLER

FOR ADDITONAL COPIES OF

HOW TO AVOID THE

C R A P

IN YOUR SEARCH FOR EMPLOYMENT!

(Click, Review, Apply & Pray)

For a quantity discount on orders of more than 30 copies,

Call 1-714-356-2239

Visa/MasterCard/AmericanExpress

theHireTarget™

FIELD TESTED EMPLOYMENT STRATEGIES

www.thehiretarget.org

www.ingramcontent.com/pod-product-compliance
Lightning Source LLC
Chambersburg PA
CBHW071645170526
45166CB00003B/1442